"ABIDING IN THE VINE– HEARING GOD'S VOICE"

7 HOUR WORKBOOK

RICHARD T. CASE

All For Jesus

Castle Rock, Colorado

ABIDING IN THE VINE: 7 HOUR WORKBOOK
7615 Lemon Gulch Way
Castle Rock, CO 80108
www.afjministy.com

Publisher's Cataloging-in-Publication data

Names:
Title:
Description: .
Identifiers: ISBN | LCCN
Subjects:

Printed in the United States of America 2020 — 1st ed

TABLE OF CONTENTS

Most Believers think that reading the Bible is important and will give us truths to live by. We tend to think that it is on us to understand it (if not, perhaps we can just get it from sermons at church or devotions from other spiritual people). We thus read it as "law" or "rules"; and it discourages us—either we really cannot understand it or seems so difficult that we cannot ever get there—so we tend to not read it regularly and thus have not found it very valuable for our everyday life. Further, since we are not in our mind spiritually mature, we do not expect to hear personally from God directly. We either disdain those who say they hear from God (Really?) or think that because I am not as spiritually mature as others, that I am not privileged to hear from God as others supposedly do. Want to, but, oh well, probably not for me. This time in the Word as a small group is intended to see how beautiful and easy it is to understand the Scriptures as God speaks them to me personally; and to regularly hear His voice. It does not require maturity at all—just a heart to hear and time with Him to hear. Stay in this Word as presented here, expect to hear, and enjoy the process of hearing.

JESUS IS OUR SHEPHERD:

Read John 10:11:

[11] I am the good shepherd. The good shepherd lays down his life for the sheep.

What is a shepherd? What does a shepherd do?

____

____

____

____

____

What kind of shepherd is Christ?

____

____

____

____

____

Why is that significant to us?

____

____

____

____

____

What does He promise us?

____

____

____

____

____

Read John 10:10:

[10] The thief comes only to steal and kill and destroy. I came that they may have life and have it abundantly.

____

____

____

____

____

Why is that significant to us?

____

____

____

____

____

As His sheep, what is our amazing privilege?

____

____

____

____

____

Read John 10:3–5; 27:

[3] To him the gatekeeper opens. The sheep hear his voice, and he calls his own sheep by name and leads them out. [4] When he has brought out all his own, he goes before them, and the sheep follow him, for they know his voice. [5] A stranger they will not follow, but they will flee from him, for they do not know the voice of strangers."

[27] My sheep hear my voice, and I know them, and they follow me.

If we are hearing His voice, what is He doing?

____

____

____

____

What are the characteristics of hearing His voice?

____

____

____

____

How will we recognize the difference between His voice and others (Satan's, ours, other people's well meaning advice)?

____

____

____

____

What is necessary to recognize His voice?

____

____

____

____

Christ is our Shepherd, and we have the privilege of hearing His voice to us personally.

What are our thoughts and experiences about hearing His voice?

____

____

____

____

AS OUR SHEPHERD, JESUS SHOWS US THE KEY TO HEARING HIS VOICE: ABIDING IN THE VINE:

Read John 15:1–5:

I Am the True Vine

15 "I am the true vine, and my Father is the vinedresser. [2] Every branch in me that does not bear fruit he takes away, and every branch that does bear fruit he prunes, that it may bear more fruit. [3] Already you are clean because of the word that I have spoken to you. [4] Abide in me, and I in you. As the branch cannot bear fruit by itself, unless it abides in the vine, neither can you, unless you abide in me. [5] I am the vine; you are the branches. Whoever abides in me and I in him, he it is that bears much fruit, for apart from me you can do nothing.

Jesus uses the analogy of a vineyard and how wine is created from all the ingredients of a vineyard. This is meant to show us the exact relationship of us to God; and how we are to hear His voice.

Describe from these verses who they are; and what role do they play in the process of us being connected to the Vine and hearing His voice:

- **The Vine:**

____

____

____

- **The Vinedresser:**

____

____

____

- **The Branch:**

____

____

____

- **The Sap (Implied):**

____

____

____

- **The Result:**

____

____

____

- **The Choice:**

____

____

____

Apart from Me, you can do _____________________.

Read John 8:28–32, 36:

28 So Jesus said to them, "When you have lifted up the Son of Man, then you will know that I am he, and that I do nothing on my own authority, but speak just as the Father taught me. 29 And he who sent me is with me. He has not left me alone, for I always do the things that are pleasing to him." 30 As he was saying these things, many believed in him.

The Truth Will Set You Free
31 So Jesus said to the Jews who had believed him, "If you abide in my word, you are truly my disciples, 32 and you will know the truth, and the truth will set you free."

36 So if the Son sets you free, you will be free indeed.

Abiding leads to _____________, which leads to _____________________.

Describe what passions we are to develop and why?

____

____

____

____

____

What is the promised outcome?

____

____

____

____

____

What does this look like in our life and why does it come to us?

____

____

____

____

____

Our role is to choose to abide—be continually and always connected to the Vine, allowing The Father to be the Vinedresser, as we receive the fruit—the wonderful results of us abiding. We are thus receivers—welcoming and processing what He has to say to us.

What are our thoughts and experiences about Abiding in the Vine (Word)?

____

____

____

____

____

HOUR 1:
HEARING HIS VOICE:

WHAT EXACTLY IS THIS FRUIT THAT COMES FROM OUR ABIDING?

- **Forgiveness:**

> **Read Romans 8:1–2:**
>
> Life in the Spirit
> **8** There is therefore now no condemnation for those who are in Christ Jesus.[a] 2 For the law of the Spirit of life has set you[b] free in Christ Jesus from the law of sin and death. What are we to fully experience as a result of being connected to the Vine?

____

____

____

____

____

If Christ does not condemn us, who else is not to condemn us? Why?

____

____

____

____

____

What is the implication of this to me personally?

____

____

____

____

____

What are we called to do with our failures and mistakes? Why?

____

____

____

____

____

Read Philippians 3:11–15:

¹¹ that by any means possible I may attain the resurrection from the dead.
Straining Toward the Goal
¹² Not that I have already obtained this or am already perfect, but I press on to make it my own, because Christ Jesus has made me his own. ¹³ Brothers, I do not consider that I have made it my own. But one thing I do: forgetting what lies behind and straining forward to what lies ahead, ¹⁴ I press on toward the goal for the prize of the upward call of God in Christ Jesus. ¹⁵ Let those of us who are mature think this way, and if in anything you think otherwise, God will reveal that also to you.

Who and what do I struggle with forgiveness?

____

____

____

____

In what areas have I not let myself off the hook and in which I continue to carry guilt?

____

____

____

____

____

- ***Unity:***

Describe from the following verses, the definition, and the value of unity? Why? What is promised to us if we live in Unity?

Read Psalm 133:

When Brothers Dwell in Unity
A Song of Ascents. Of David.
133 Behold, how good and pleasant it is
    when brothers dwell in unity![a]
2 It is like the precious oil on the head,
    running down on the beard,
on the beard of Aaron,
    running down on the collar of his robes!
3 It is like the dew of Hermon,
    which falls on the mountains of Zion!
For there the Lord has commanded the blessing,
    life forevermore.

____

____

____

____

____

____

Read Ecclesiastes 4:9–12:

9 Two are better than one, because they have a good reward for their toil. 10 For if they fall, one will lift up his fellow. But woe to him who is alone when he falls and has not another to lift him up! 11 Again, if two lie together, they keep warm, but how can one keep warm alone? 12 And though a man might prevail against one who is alone, two will withstand him—a threefold cord is not quickly broken.

Read Ephesians 4:1–6:

Unity in the Body of Christ

4 I therefore, a prisoner for the Lord, urge you to walk in a manner worthy of the calling to which you have been called, [2] with all humility and gentleness, with patience, bearing with one another in love, [3] eager to maintain the unity of the Spirit in the bond of peace. [4] There is one body and one Spirit—just as you were called to the one hope that belongs to your call— [5] one Lord, one faith, one baptism, [6] one God and Father of all, who is over all and through all and in all.

What is the reason we can get to unity every time, all the time?

____

____

____

____

____

How am I doing at unity with my spouse or close friends (if not married)? Why or why not?

____

____

____

____

____

What is required for me to adjust my approach with my spouse or close friends (if not married) to reach the unity promised by God?

- *Joy:*

From the following verses, describe what it means to have joy? What are keys to receiving and living out joy?

Read Psalm 128:

Blessed Is Everyone Who Fears the Lord
A Song of Ascents.
128 Blessed is everyone who fears the Lord,
  who walks in his ways!
2 You shall eat the fruit of the labor of your hands;
   you shall be blessed, and it shall be well with you.
3 Your wife will be like a fruitful vine
   within your house;
your children will be like olive shoots
   around your table.
4 Behold, thus shall the man be blessed
   who fears the Lord.
5 The Lord bless you from Zion!
  May you see the prosperity of Jerusalem
  all the days of your life!
6 May you see your children's children!
   Peace be upon Israel!

Read Ecclesiastes 9:7–10:

Enjoy Life with the One You Love
7 Go, eat your bread with joy, and drink your wine with a merry heart, for God has already approved what you do.

8 Let your garments be always white. Let not oil be lacking on your head.
9 Enjoy life with the wife whom you love, all the days of your vain[a] life that he has given you under the sun, because that is your portion in life and in your toil at which you toil under the sun. 10 Whatever your hand finds to do, do it with your might[b] for there is no work or thought or knowledge or wisdom in Sheol, to which you are going.

How would I describe the amount of joy I normally experience in my life? Why or why not?

- ***Led by Spirit:***

From the following verses, describe the work of the Holy Spirit in our lives. How are we to respond?

> **Read Romans 8:12–17:**
>
> Heirs with Christ
> [12] So then, brothers,[a] we are debtors, not to the flesh, to live according to the flesh.[13] For if you live according to the flesh you will die, but if by the Spirit you put to death the deeds of the body, you will live. [14] For all who are led by the Spirit of God are sons[b]of God. [15] For you did not receive the spirit of slavery to fall back into fear, but you have received the Spirit of adoption as sons, by whom we cry, "Abba! Father!" [16] The Spirit himself bears witness with our spirit that we are children of God, [17] and if children, then heirs—heirs of God and fellow heirs with Christ, provided we suffer with him in order that we may also be glorified with him.

> **Read John 16:13–15:**
>
> [13] When the Spirit of truth comes, he will guide you into all the truth, for he will not speak on his own authority, but whatever he hears he will speak, and he will declare to you the things that are to come. [14] He will glorify me, for he will take what is mine and declare it to you. [15] All that the Father has is mine; therefore I said that he will take what is mine and declare it to you.

Do I regularly experience being led by the Holy Spirit or does this seem like a distant possibility for me? Why or why not?

____

____

____

____

____

- ***Character Transformation:***

> **Read Galatians 5:22–25:**
>
> [22] But the fruit of the Spirit is love, joy, peace, patience, kindness, goodness, faithfulness,[23] gentleness, self-control; against such things there is no law. [24] And those who belong to Christ Jesus have crucified the flesh with its passions and desires.
>
> [25] If we live by the Spirit, let us also keep in step with the Spirit.
> What are the elements of our character transformation?

____

____

____

____

____

Why is our character transformation so important to our life in God as His sheep? How would we know?

____

____

____

____

Would my spouse or my friends (if not married) say I that my character is being transformed? Why or why not?

____

____

____

____

____

- ***Answered Prayers:***

From the following verses, what promises of answered prayers are available to us? Why is this so significant to us?

> **Read 2 Corinthians 1:18–22:**
>
> [18] As surely as God is faithful, our word to you has not been Yes and No. [19] For the Son of God, Jesus Christ, whom we proclaimed among you, Silvanus and Timothy and I, was not Yes and No, but in him it is always Yes. [20] For all the promises of God find their Yes in him. That is why it is through him that we utter our Amen to God for his glory. [21] And it is God who establishes us with you in Christ, and has anointed us, [22] and who has also put his seal on us and given us his Spirit in our hearts as a guarantee.[a]

> **Read John 15:7–8:**
>
> [7] If you abide in me, and my words abide in you, ask whatever you wish, and it will be done for you. [8] By this my Father is glorified, that you bear much fruit and so prove to be my disciples.

("Word" here is "Rhema"—His application of the Written Word (Logos) to us personally.)

____

____

____

____

What are the conditions to answered prayer?

____

____

____

____

Am I seeing wonderful answers to prayer? Why or why not?

____

____

____

____

- ***Desires of your heart:***

> **Read Psalm 37:3–8:**
>
> [3] Trust in the Lord, and do good;
> dwell in the land and befriend faithfulness.[a]
> [4] Delight yourself in the Lord,
> and he will give you the desires of your heart.
> [5] Commit your way to the Lord;
> trust in him, and he will act.
> [6] He will bring forth your righteousness as the light,
> and your justice as the noonday.
> [7] Be still before the Lord and wait patiently for him;
> fret not yourself over the one who prospers in his way,
> over the man who carries out evil devices!
> [8] Refrain from anger, and forsake wrath!
> Fret not yourself; it tends only to evil.

What does God promise us? What are the conditions to this promise? How do we practically meet these conditions?

____

____

____

____

____

____

Write out the true desires of your heart—your dreams. Do not censure nor qualify—just write in as much detail as possible your desires. During this next week, process these with your spouse or another friend (if not married). Begin praying together that you can meet the conditions and God will deliver on His promise.

WHAT ARE THE KEYS TO RECEIVING THIS FRUIT?

- ***Enjoying the Abiding:***

From the following verses, what is important in the process (the how) of abiding and receiving the promised fruit?

Read Luke 10:38–42:

Martha and Mary
38 Now as they went on their way, Jesus[a] entered a village. And a woman named Martha welcomed him into her house. 39 And she had a sister called Mary, who sat at the Lord's feet and listened to his teaching. 40 But Martha was distracted with much serving. And she went up to him and said, "Lord, do you not care that my sister has left me to serve alone? Tell her then to help me." 41 But the Lord answered her, "Martha, Martha, you are anxious and troubled about many things, 42 but one thing is necessary.[b] Mary has chosen the good portion, which will not be taken away from her."

What is the difference between Martha and Mary? What does Christ say about this? Why?

____

____

____

____

____

____

____

Read Proverbs 4:1–7; 20–23:

A Father's Wise Instruction
4 Hear, O sons, a father's instruction,
 and be attentive, that you may gain[a] insight,
2 for I give you good precepts;
 do not forsake my teaching.
3 When I was a son with my father,
 tender, the only one in the sight of my mother,
4 he taught me and said to me,
"Let your heart hold fast my words;
 keep my commandments, and live.
5 Get wisdom; get insight;
 do not forget, and do not turn away from the words of my mouth.
6 Do not forsake her, and she will keep you;
 love her, and she will guard you.
7 The beginning of wisdom is this: Get wisdom,
 and whatever you get, get insight.

20 My son, be attentive to my words;
 incline your ear to my sayings.
21 Let them not escape from your sight;
 keep them within your heart.
22 For they are life to those who find them,
 and healing to all their[a] flesh.
23 Keep your heart with all vigilance,
 for from it flow the springs of life.

What is necessary for the Word to become real and powerful in our lives? How does this practically work?

____

____

____

____

____

____

How does this work, and what does this mean in terms of practicing this every day?

____

____

____

____

____

Read Jeremiah 15:16:

16 Your words were found, and I ate them,
   and your words became to me a joy
   and the delight of my heart,
for I am called by your name,
   O Lord, God of hosts.

Read Luke 2:41–52:

The Boy Jesus in the Temple

41 Now his parents went to Jerusalem every year at the Feast of the Passover. 42 And when he was twelve years old, they went up according to custom. 43 And when the feast was ended, as they were returning, the boy Jesus stayed behind in Jerusalem. His parents did not know it, 44 but supposing him to be in the group they went a day's journey, but then they began to search for him among their relatives and acquaintances, 45 and when they did not find him, they returned to Jerusalem, searching for him. 46 After three days they found him in the temple, sitting among the teachers, listening to them and asking them questions. 47 And all who heard him were amazed at his understanding and his answers. 48 And when his parents[a] saw him, they were astonished. And his mother said to him, "Son, why have you treated us so? Behold, your father and I have been searching for you in great distress." 49 And he said to them, "Why were you looking for me? Did you not know that I must be in my Father's house?"[b] 50 And they did not understand the saying that he spoke to them. 51 And he went down with them and came to Nazareth and was submissive to them. And his mother treasured up all these things in her heart.

52 And Jesus increased in wisdom and in stature[c] and in favor with God and man.

Is this way of abiding in the Word regularly happening in my life? Why or why not?

Read through and discuss the following instructions on Abiding in the Word:

ABIDING IN THE WORD

1. Pursue your interest; what interesting Word or thought that the Spirit has been piquing your interest; what you already know God is laying on your heart.

2. Write out the specific Scriptures—Recommend a good Cross Reference Study Bible with helps and concordance: NKJV (Spirit Filled Life Bible is particularly good as it includes translations of Greek and Hebrew words); NASB; NEV; Amplified—and do not use paraphrase as primary Bible, only as some additional help. Can go to www.biblegateway.com or www.crosswalk.com for different translations. Spend some time understanding the context of the specific Bible Book from which the verse is taken. Also, do not read just the specific verse, but read the entire paragraph for context.

3. Cross reference specific verses by using your Cross Reference Study Bible which will take you to other truth about that particular revelation; and perform Word studies using concordance at back of your bible or www.biblegateway.com or www.crosswalk.com. As you spend time in the cross-referenced or word study verses, let the "quickening" of the Spirit lead you regarding whether this is something He is speaking to you; and only then spend time further processing. If it does not strike your heart much, do not spend any further time on it and continue to cross reference other verses that strike your heart or go to another verse from your Word study.

4. Write out your thoughts about:

    a. What this says about the character of God?
    b. What God has done, is doing or promises to do?
    c. Are there any conditions to what God promises? (If…then)
    d. What are my responsibilities or responses?

5. Go deeper into Hebrew and Greek meaning of the Words He is speaking to you: (www.crosswalk.com, click on "Bible Study Tools" at top of website, center right; then on next screen click on "Interlinear

Bible"—type in word or verses: when the verses come up along with the Greek & Hebrew on the next screen, click on your chosen word, then from the next screen, print the Hebrew or Greek word meanings.

6. Memorize the verses (word for word)—carry 3x5 cards with you.

7. Journal your thoughts:

    a. Do I believe this in my heart (is it settled?) why or why not? (What do I struggle with & what experiences in my life, work against what I am receiving in the Word?)
    b. How do these words apply to my situation and me?
    c. How is God calling me to adjust my life to Him and His will?
    d. What thoughts come to me about all this?
    e. Dialogue with the Father your thoughts. Ask for clarity, understanding, wisdom, faith.

8. Pray the promises: Ask God to fulfill what He has said to you.

9. Commit time with a friend or spouse, sharing your journal—what God is saying to you.

    a. Discuss feelings, reactions, & insights—why important to me.
    b. Study specific verses that each is sharing.
    c. Pray verses together.

- *How does this process of God speaking to us and us getting His Words in our hearts actually happen?*

From the following verses, what must we understand and then practice to continually hear from God and respond in obedience?

> **Read 1 Corinthians 2:9–12:**
>
> [9] But, as it is written,
> "What no eye has seen, nor ear heard,
>   nor the heart of man imagined,
> what God has prepared for those who love him"—
> [10] these things God has revealed to us through the Spirit. For the Spirit

searches everything, even the depths of God. [11] For who knows a person's thoughts except the spirit of that person, which is in him? So also no one comprehends the thoughts of God except the Spirit of God. [12] Now we have received not the spirit of the world, but the Spirit who is from God, that we might understand the things freely given us by God.

Why cannot we do this with our own senses, intellect and logic?

____

____

____

____

What has the Father already done and what is His role? What is our role?

____

____

____

____

Read 2 Corinthians 3:4–6; 16–18:

[4] Such is the confidence that we have through Christ toward God. [5] Not that we are sufficient in ourselves to claim anything as coming from us, but our sufficiency is from God, [6] who has made us sufficient to be ministers of a new covenant, not of the letter but of the Spirit. For the letter kills, but the Spirit gives life.

[16] But when one[a] turns to the Lord, the veil is removed. [17] Now the Lord[b] is the Spirit, and where the Spirit of the Lord is, there is freedom. [18] And we all, with unveiled face, beholding the glory of the Lord,[c] are being transformed into the same image from one degree of glory to another.[d] For this comes from the Lord who is the Spirit.

Whose sufficiency do we rely upon in this process? Why is that most important and what is the good news of this?

____

____

____

____

____

What happens when we read the Scripture as law and rules? Why?
What happens when we allow the Spirit to speak life from the Words to us? Why?

____

____

____

____

____

In verses 16–18: What is Christ's objective for us as we abide? Define what this looks like?

____

____

____

____

____

What is promised of what happens where the Spirit is operating in our life? Define what this looks like?

____

____

____

____

____

Does it happen after we are being transformed, or during the journey? Why is this important?

____

____

____

____

____

Read Mark 4:13–20:

[13] And he said to them, "Do you not understand this parable? How then will you understand all the parables? [14] The sower sows the word. [15] And these are the ones along the path, where the word is sown: when they hear, Satan immediately comes and takes away the word that is sown in them. [16] And these are the ones sown on rocky ground: the ones who, when they hear the word, immediately receive it with joy. [17] And they have no root in themselves, but endure for a while; then, when tribulation or persecution arises on account of the word, immediately they fall away.[a] [18] And others are the ones sown among thorns. They are those who hear the word, [19] but the cares of the world and the deceitfulness of riches and the desires for other things enter in and choke the word, and it proves unfruitful. [20] But those that were sown on the good soil are the ones who hear the word and accept it and bear fruit, thirtyfold and sixtyfold and a hundredfold."

What is the key to receiving and experiencing the promised fruit of abiding?
How does this practically work?

____

____

____

____

____

Understand that it is spiritual (we subordinate our intellect to the Spirit), as receiving process, a process of joy and life.

We are to share and process together what we are learning with our spouse and other spiritual believers.

What is necessary to soften up my heart and prepare the "soil" to welcome and understand the Word in my life?

____

____

____

____

____

The Spirit speaks to us from the written Word (Logos) as He applies it to our individual lives (Rhema) by making it life (stimulating, interesting, attractive, powerful, & vibrant). He has prepared in advance what He wishes to reveal to us.

The Keys are to be in the Word where He is speaking life to us, processing deeper until it gets into the midst of our heart (takes time, journaling, memorizing, enjoying the life—there is no rush or need for quantity).

Let's summarize now how this process all works.

1. *Christ is our Shepherd, and we have the privilege of hearing His voice to us personally.*

2. *The Spirit speaks to us from the written Word (Logos) as He applies it to our individual lives (Rhema) by making it life (stimulating, interesting, attractive, powerful, & vibrant). He has prepared in advance what He wishes to reveal to us.*

3. *Our role is to choose to abide—be continually and always connected to the Vine, allowing The Father to be the Vinedresser, as we receive the fruit—the wonderful results of us abiding. We are thus receivers—welcoming and processing what He has to say to us.*

4. *The Keys are to be in the Word where He is speaking life to us, processing deeper until it gets into the midst of our heart (takes time, journaling, memorizing, enjoying the life—there is no rush or need for quantity).*

5. *Understand that it is spiritual (we subordinate our intellect to the Spirit), as receiving process, a process of joy and life.*

6. *We are to share and process together what we are learning with our spouse and other spiritual believers.*

7. *The Father desires that His Rhema Word to us results in faith—we believe it, live it and then experience it in our real lives.*

8. *Remember the Spirit is guiding the whole process—He speaks through the Word and leads our steps each day.*

1. EXERCISE IN ABIDING AND HEARING HIS VOICE: WHAT DOES THE FATHER HAVE TO SAY TO YOU?

Read Ezekiel 34:11-30:

The Lord God Will Seek Them Out

11 "For thus says the Lord God: Behold, I, I myself will search for my sheep and will seek them out. 12 As a shepherd seeks out his flock when he is among his sheep that have been scattered, so will I seek out my sheep, and I will rescue them from all places where they have been scattered on a day of clouds and thick darkness. 13 And I will bring them out from the peoples and gather them from the countries, and will bring them into their own land. And I will feed them on the mountains of Israel, by the ravines, and in all the inhabited places of the country. 14 I will feed them with good pasture, and on the mountain heights of Israel shall be their grazing land. There they shall lie down in good grazing land, and on rich pasture they shall feed on the mountains of Israel. 15 I myself will be the shepherd of my sheep, and I myself will make them lie down, declares the Lord God. 16 I will seek the lost, and I will bring back the strayed, and I will bind up the injured, and I will strengthen the weak, and the fat and the strong I will destroy.[a] I will feed them in justice.

17 "As for you, my flock, thus says the Lord God: Behold, I judge between sheep and sheep, between rams and male goats. 18 Is it not enough for you to feed on the good pasture, that you must tread down with your feet the rest of your pasture; and to drink of clear water, that you must muddy the rest of the water with your feet? 19 And must my sheep eat what you have trodden with your feet, and drink what you have muddied with your feet?

20 "Therefore, thus says the Lord God to them: Behold, I, I myself will judge between the fat sheep and the lean sheep. 21 Because

you push with side and shoulder, and thrust at all the weak with your horns, till you have scattered them abroad, [22] I will rescue[b] my flock; they shall no longer be a prey. And I will judge between sheep and sheep. [23] And I will set up over them one shepherd, my servant David, and he shall feed them: he shall feed them and be their shepherd. [24] And I, the Lord, will be their God, and my servant David shall be prince among them. I am the Lord; I have spoken.

The Lord's Covenant of Peace

[25] "I will make with them a covenant of peace and banish wild beasts from the land, so that they may dwell securely in the wilderness and sleep in the woods. [26] And I will make them and the places all around my hill a blessing, and I will send down the showers in their season; they shall be showers of blessing. [27] And the trees of the field shall yield their fruit, and the earth shall yield its increase, and they shall be secure in their land. And they shall know that I am the Lord, when I break the bars of their yoke, and deliver them from the hand of those who enslaved them. [28] They shall no more be a prey to the nations, nor shall the beasts of the land devour them. They shall dwell securely, and none shall make them afraid. [29] And I will provide for them renowned plantations so that they shall no more be consumed with hunger in the land, and no longer suffer the reproach of the nations. 30 And they shall know that I am the Lord their God with them, and that they, the house of Israel, are my people, declares the Lord God.

Identify one to three of God's promises as our Shepherd ("I will"). Let the Spirit impress upon you the one that He wants to speak to you today. Write what this promise means to you and why is the Lord promising this to you. Then cross reference this verse to another promise (another verse—remember to spend time working thru the entire paragraph of the cross reference) of God in Scripture and write what this means to you and why the Lord is promising this to you. Then, again cross reference that verse and do the same.

____

____

____

____

____

Let's summarize again how this process all works.

1. Christ is our Shepherd, and we have the privilege of hearing His voice to us personally.

2. The Spirit speaks to us from the written Word (Logos) as He applies it to our individual lives (Rhema) by making it life (stimulating, interesting, attractive, powerful, & vibrant). He has prepared in advance what He wishes to reveal to us.

3. Our role is to choose to abide—be continually and always connected to the Vine, allowing The Father to be the Vinedresser, as we receive the fruit –the wonderful results of us abiding. We are thus receivers—welcoming and processing what He has to say to us.

4. The Keys are to be in the Word where He is speaking life to us, processing deeper until it gets into the midst of our heart (takes time, journaling, memorizing, enjoying the life—there is no rush or need for quantity).

5. Understand that it is spiritual (we subordinate our intellect to the Spirit), as receiving process, a process of joy and life.

6. We are to share and process together what we are learning with our spouse and other spiritual believers.

7. The Father desires that His Rhema Word to us results in faith—we believe it, live it and then experience it in our real lives.

8. Remember the Spirit is guiding the whole process—He speaks through the Word and leads our steps each day.

Practice now what you have learned—staying abiding and enjoy hearing from God!